People at Work

Working on a Farm

by Connor Stratton

FOCUS READERS®

SCOUT

www.focusreaders.com

Focus Readers is distributed by North Star Editions:
sales@northstareditions.com | 888-417-0195

Produced for Focus Readers by Red Line Editorial.

Photographs ©: andresr/iStockphoto, cover, 1; stevanovicigor/iStockphoto, 4 (top); chonticha stocker/Shutterstock Images, 4 (bottom); vgajic/iStockphoto, 7 (top), 16 (top right); Torwaistudio/Shutterstock Images, 7 (bottom), 16 (top left); oticki/Shutterstock Images, 9 (top); Sasa Prudkov/Shutterstock Images, 9 (bottom); Iakov Filimonov/ Shutterstock Images, 11; PeopleImages/iStockphoto, 13 (top); greenaperture/Shutterstock Images, 13 (bottom); JuneChalida/Shutterstock Images, 15; LightField Studios/ Shutterstock Images, 16 (bottom left); Emjay Smith/Shutterstock Images, 16 (bottom right)

Library of Congress Cataloging-in-Publication Data
Names: Stratton, Connor, author.
Title: Working on a farm / by Connor Stratton.
Description: Lake Elmo, MN : Focus Readers, [2020] | Series: People at work | Includes index. | Audience: Grades K–1
Identifiers: LCCN 2019032481 (print) | LCCN 2019032482 (ebook) | ISBN 9781644930182 (hardcover) | ISBN 9781644930977 (paperback) | ISBN 9781644932551 (pdf) | ISBN 9781644931769 (ebook)
Subjects: LCSH: Farmers--Juvenile literature. | Agriculture--Juvenile literature.
Classification: LCC S519 .S78 2020 (print) | LCC S519 (ebook) | DDC 630--dc23
LC record available at https://lccn.loc.gov/2019032481
LC ebook record available at https://lccn.loc.gov/2019032482

Printed in the United States of America
Mankato, MN
012020

About the Author

Connor Stratton enjoys cooking food, eating vegetables, and watching movies with friends. He lives in Minnesota.

Table of Contents

On the Farm 5

Planting and Feeding 8

Making Food 12

Glossary 16

Index 16

On the Farm

Many people work
on farms.
Some **farmers** grow crops.
Crops grow in fields.

Some farmers raise animals.

They may raise chickens.

They may raise **cows**.

chicken

cow

Planting and Feeding

Farmers plant seeds.

They use **tractors**.

They water the fields.

Water helps seeds grow.

tractor

water

Farmers feed animals.

They feed cows.

Cows eat hay.

Hay helps cows grow.

hay

Making Food

Farmers pick crops.

They pick vegetables.

They pick wheat.

vegetable

wheat

Chickens lay **eggs**.

Farmers gather eggs.

Farmers make food

for people.

egg

Glossary

cows

farmers

eggs

tractors

Index

C

chickens, 6, 14

E

eggs, 14

T

tractors, 8

W

wheat, 12